IMMUNE
TO
DISEASE

Enjoying divine health and healing

ISAAC ESSILFIE

BOOKS BY ISAAC ESSILFIE

Incorruptible Series:

➤ Incorruptible Book #1: The realm of the mind
➤ Incorruptible Book #2: Steadfast & immovable amidst the darkness of this present world

Daily Glory Series:

➤ How to Pray: The dimensions of operation in prayer
➤ How to walk in grace and favour daily
➤ Manifesting your heavenly inheritance

➤ Loving by loving yourself
➤ The Spirit of Christ
➤ The New Creature: Life from Death
➤ Immune to Disease: Enjoying divine health and healing

To the reader

Scripture references in this book are taken from the King James Version (KJV) of the bible.

Table of Contents

WHAT IS A DISEASE?

Diseases come after the life of the body. There is only one spirit being who mobilizes other spirit beings to destroy God's creation; the Devil. He is the one who comes to steal, kill and destroy. He teaches men how to destroy themselves and uses their resources against them. He is the one who comes after the bodies of men using his devices.

Sickness and diseases may appear physical but they are manifestations of the thoughts of the devil to destroy the bodies of men. You can never be entirely free from them by medical interventions. There is always a disease to handle the strongest of immune systems and some of these diseases cannot be cured. Diseases cannot be flashed out of the earth using physical interventions because of their spiritual element.

"And, behold, there was a woman which had a spirit of infirmity eighteen years, and was bowed together, and could in no wise lift up herself.

And when Jesus saw her, he called her to him, and said unto her, Woman, thou art loosed from thine infirmity.

And he laid his hands on her: and immediately she was made straight, and glorified God." (Luke 13:11-13)

You cannot really be careful enough when it comes to diseases. No matter what you do, a virus or bacteria will definitely come into contact with your body so long as you are in this world. They are microscopic and cannot be utterly avoided. It is impossible to take a defensive measure against what you cannot even see. It is better to be above those devices to live freely.

Fortunately, that is what you have been made in Christ Jesus, and you must walk in that life by the practice of the given knowledge.

WHAT DOES IT MEAN TO BELIEVE?

This is where the misunderstanding mostly lies. Believing to some people means to merely think to be true; that is not what the bible says about it. To believe according to the scriptures is to act on information that the word of God provides which you have accepted. You can feel something is true, like it, want it or even agree with it, once you do not act based on the instruction of the word of God concerning it, you have not believed. You can agree with the gospel of Jesus Christ preached to you, like it, enjoy it or even feel good about it but if you do not open your mouth to say what you are required to say, you have still not believed.

Until you open your mouth to say you believe, you have not believed. Your confession is the declaration of your belief.

"But what saith it? The word is nigh thee, even in thy mouth, and in thy heart: that is, the word of faith, which we preach;

That if thou shalt confess with thy mouth the Lord Jesus, and shalt believe in thine heart that God hath raised him from the dead, thou shalt be saved.

For with the heart man believeth unto righteousness; and with the mouth confession is made unto salvation."

(Romans 10:8-10)

"Jesus said unto him, If thou canst believe, all things are possible to him that believeth.

And straightway the father of the child cried out, and said with tears, Lord, I believe; help thou mine unbelief."

(Mark 9:23-24)

You are a believer for hearing and acting on the word, not merely thinking the word to be true.

THESE SIGNS SHALL FOLLOW THEM THAT BELIEVE

And he said unto them, Go ye into all the world, and preach the gospel to every creature.

He that believeth and is baptized shall be saved; but he that believeth not shall be damned.

And these signs shall follow them that believe; In my name shall they cast out devils; they shall speak with new tongues;

They shall take up serpents; and if they drink any deadly thing, it shall not hurt them; they shall lay hands on the sick, and they shall recover.

(Mark 16:15-18)

For anyone who believes the gospel of salvation, these are the first signs to be seen. Note that Jesus did not put a name to it, He only said those who believe.

These cannot work for you until you have opened your mouth to say you believe. You are not a believer until you have said you believe in the Lord Jesus Christ.

If your salvation was by your testimony based on the gospel of salvation which you received, every other thing it has to offer follows that pattern.

These signs have been said concerning those who would come to believe by the hearing of the gospel of salvation. In other words, you must identify yourself as the one who has believed, the one of whom Jesus spoke. This is the first way to do the word.

Lord I believe, these signs follow me because I have believed. I cast out devils, I speak with tongues, I pick up serpents, harmful substances do

not work in my body, I lay hands on the sick, and
they recover.

Remember that you have been able to speak in
tongues since you believed. This is an indication
that all those signs mentioned are as basic as the
tongues you speak. These are the first signs that
should follow you when you come to believe.

HE QUICKENS YOUR
MORTAL BODY

But if the Spirit of him that raised up Jesus from the dead dwell in you, he that raised up Christ from the dead shall also quicken your mortal bodies by his Spirit that dwelleth in you. (Romans 8:11)

The Holy Ghost dwells in you because you are a believer. He was in Christ and He is in anyone who has come to believe in Christ Jesus. He is the power of God in your spirit and He vitalizes your mortal body. He is the reason why your body can be immune to diseases. The power of God in you is stronger than any spiritual device created to destroy your body.

The Holy Ghost keeps your body immune by supplying power to your body. That power is called Dunamis, it keeps your body in a constant state of health beyond what medical interventions can provide. With that power running through your body, no virus, bacteria or disease can work in your body. It will not survive. It does not matter if it got inside you by mistake or deliberately, it will not work.

"They shall take up serpents; **and if they drink any deadly thing, it shall not hurt them**; they shall lay hands on the sick, and they shall recover."
(Mark 16:18)

This is what God has done to keep you free from diseases in this world; He places spiritual immunity inside you by the Holy Ghost given unto you. In order for the power of the Holy Ghost to work inside you, He needs the word of God in you.

MEDITATION

This book of the law shall not depart out of thy mouth; but thou shalt meditate therein day and night, that thou mayest observe to do according to all that is written therein: for then thou shalt make thy way prosperous, and then thou shalt have good success.
(Joshua 1:8)

"But his delight is in the law of the LORD; and in his law doth he meditate day and night."
(Psalms 1:2)

"I will meditate also of all thy work, and talk of thy doings."
(Psalms 77:12)

"I will meditate in thy precepts, and have respect unto thy ways."

(Psalms 119:15)

"Meditate upon these things; give thyself wholly to them; that thy profiting may appear to all."

(1 Timothy 4:15)

Meditation is not sitting down quietly thinking about the word of God. It is the repetition of the word of God in your mouth so that it enters your heart. To meditate on the word of God means to speak the word of God repeatedly to yourself in your closet, it is the keeping of the word of God in your heart.

The word of God you hear or read is of no use to you if it has not entered your spirit. All the saints who manifested the power of God meditated on the word of God as the scriptures reveal.

The word of God concerning your immunity to diseases and any deadly thing entering the body is for your meditation, not mere reading. Those words must enter you.

You say them to yourself in your closet over and over again. In each session, you can start with just 10 minutes for each line:

I cast out devils

Deadly things do not harm me, diseases have no place in my body.

I am the one who lays hands on the sick for them to recover.

I am the one who picks up serpents.

I believe in the Lord Jesus Christ, and these signs follow me.

My body is energized by the power of the Holy Ghost resident in me.

The Spirit of him that raised Jesus from the dead dwells in me, my outer body is vitalized.

I am immune to the devices of the enemy against the body because the Holy Ghost dwells in me.

THE BODY OF THE HOLY GHOST

The Holy Ghost is the power of God inside you. He is the life of God inside you. He is the life of the word of God in you. He is the one who makes alive the word of God to you. The word of God tells Him what He should be and what He should produce inside you. Without the word of God, He does not know what He should be. It is the word of God concerning healing that makes Him work as the healing power of God unto you. The word of God directs and instructs Him, it brings Him into action.

"For who hath known the mind of the Lord, that he may instruct him? But we have the mind of Christ."

(1 Corinthians 2:16)

The word of God you push inside you through meditation gives the Holy Ghost a form; a body. The word of God gives Him an identity; it gives Him what He should be. The word of God is His transportation.

"In the beginning God created the heaven and the earth.

And the earth was without form, and void; and darkness was upon the face of the deep. And the Spirit of God moved upon the face of the waters.

And God said, Let there be light: and there was light."

(Genesis 1:1-3)

The Holy Ghost does not know what to do except the word of God tells Him. Until the word of God went forth, He was hovering over the surface of the deep. He did not act, He did not create, He did not perform.

The word of God that enters you through meditation lets Him know what He is to be as the Spirit of God inside you. Without the word of God, you will never experience any operation of Holy Ghost whatsoever. The word of God concerning the signs that should follow you as a believer tells the Holy Ghost to function as the power of God inside you that gives vitality to your body. He can now identify as the power of God inside you.

THE QUICKENING OF
THE SPIRIT

It is the spirit that quickeneth; the flesh profiteth nothing: the words that I speak unto you, they are spirit, and they are life. (John 6:63)

The word of God gives the Holy Ghost an identity inside you. Now the words you speak, they are spirit, and they are life. This is not meditation but the declaration of the word of God that has entered you. Those words now go forth as the power of the Holy Ghost that quickens your body. When Jesus spoke before the people, that was not meditation. He was speaking the word of God in Him to the people and that He called spirit and life.

After you have spent time to meditate on the word of God concerning the signs that should follow you as a believer, you say:

I am healthy, the power of the Holy Ghost runs through my body.

In the name of Jesus, you devil, get out of this body. (that is if you or another is sick)

I am/you are healed by the power of the Holy Ghost. (that is if you or another is sick)

You can now instruct the Holy Ghost inside you because the word of God He needs to function has been made available through meditation. This is when the Holy Ghost works as the power of God in your body. The word of God you declare is His vehicle for the operation which you have pronounced. It is as basic as the tongues you speak.

Now you can cast out devils, keep healthy and heal others because those words have entered you. The word of God inside you goes forth as the instruction of the Holy Ghost unto operation.

"For who hath known the mind of the Lord, that he may instruct him? But we have the mind of Christ."

(1 Corinthians 2:16)

Jesus spent time feeding on the word of God and He came out working miracles. He said it was the Father in Him (the Holy Ghost) doing those works.

"Believest thou not that I am in the Father, and the Father in me? the words that I speak unto you I speak not of myself: but the Father that dwelleth in me, he doeth the works."

(John 14:10)

The Holy Ghost was the doer of the works that Jesus did. He only needed to take in the word of God and speak it when needed for the Holy Ghost to do. This is a pattern revealed in the scriptures to be used.

THE WORD OF GOD IN YOUR MOUTH IS LIFE

The word of God in your mouth is life when those words come from inside you. Speaking forth the word of God which is not inside you means the Holy Ghost does not have what it takes to perform that instruction. He cannot be unto you what you say without the word inside you.

"It is the spirit that quickeneth; the flesh profiteth nothing: the words that I speak unto you, they are spirit, and they are life." (John 6:63)

CAST OUT DEVILS, SPIRITUAL IMMUNITY

This is not just about people possessed with devils. The devices of the enemy also need to be driven out. If any disease finds its way into your body or you are to heal another who is sick, remember it is a spiritual device. As such, you drive it out of the body knowing it is a spirit of infirmity. You say:

In the name of Jesus, you devil, get out of this body.

Having done that, touch or stretch forth your hand towards the sick or yourself and say:

You are healed by the power of the Holy Ghost.

You can also speak to the particular part of the body suffering from the disease saying:

Be made whole, by the power of the Holy Ghost.

SPEAKING IN TONGUES

As you speak in tongues, declare the word of God, the instruction of the Holy Ghost concerning the spiritual immunity of your body.

I am vitalized by the power of the Holy Ghost.

My body is quickened by the power of the Holy Ghost.

When you speak in tongues, it is your spirit giving expression to the word of God which you have received in its raw form; spirit. You speak healing, joy, peace and marvellous things of God. You are not speaking them into occurrence, you are revealing or giving expression to the word of God in your spirit.

In this case, your tongues testify of your authority, your spiritual immunity, your ability to shutter the devices of the enemy. It is your spirit mentioning the word of God that has entered your heart exactly as it is, not in human language.

The vocabulary of your tongues increases as more of the word of God enters your spirit. Once you spend time to speak in tongues, more words come out of your spirit as the word of God gives your spirit expression.

Speaking in tongues is your spirit speaking the word of God without using human language.

"And they were all filled with the Holy Ghost, and began to speak with other tongues, as the Spirit gave them utterance.

And there were dwelling at Jerusalem Jews, devout men, out of every nation under heaven.

Now when this was noised abroad, the multitude came together, and were confounded, because that every man heard them speak in his own language.

And they were all amazed and marvelled, saying one to another, Behold, are not all these which speak Galilaeans?

And how hear we every man in our own tongue, wherein we were born?

Parthians, and Medes, and Elamites, and the dwellers in Mesopotamia, and in Judaea, and Cappadocia, in Pontus, and Asia,

Phrygia, and Pamphylia, in Egypt, and in the parts of Libya about Cyrene, and strangers of Rome, Jews and proselytes,

Cretes and Arabians, we do hear them speak in our tongues the wonderful works of God.

And they were all amazed, and were in doubt, saying one to another, What meaneth this?"

(Acts 2:4-12)

Speaking in tongues stirs up energy inside your spirit and it has to be accompanied by instruction of the word of God to release that energy as the power of God that quickens your body. Anytime you pray in tongues, you must declare the word of God. The tongue is a testimony of the word of God inside you and your declaration is the word of God going forth as the power of the Holy Ghost to perform as the word says.

As you speak in tongues and are stirred up in spirit, you say:

I am vitalized by the power of the Holy Ghost.

My body is quickened by the power of the Holy Ghost.

I heal the sick. I lay hands on the sick and they recover.

I pick up serpents and they cannot harm me.

Poison does not work in my body.

My body is refreshed every day, my body is vitalized every day, by the power of the Holy Ghost.

Amen.

INCORRUPTIBLE (BOOK 1)

Finally, my brethren, be strong in the Lord, and in the power of his might.
Put on the whole armour of God, that ye may be able to stand against the wiles of the devil.
(Ephesians 6:10-11)

This is not a matter of being religious or spiritual; the fact is that there are schemes in operation in this world. Some of these schemes are man-made while most of them are influenced by unseen factors. People find this difficult to accept but are able to relate to unseen things such as love. Love, an unseen substance or condition, is able to make people do things they would not do under normal circumstances. It makes them look like they are being blinded and controlled.

Anyone able to understand this should not find it too wonderful to believe that there are schemes at work in this world not just by men.

INCORRUPTIBLE

The Realm of the Mind

ISAAC ESSILFIE

Search **Incorruptible book 1 by Isaac Essilfie**
on Amazon to get this book.

NOTE FROM THE AUTHOR

Thanks for spending time to read my book.
I'd be glad if you would:

Review this book
Enjoyed this book? Why not post a review on AMAZON even if a brief one?

Spread the word
Liked this book? Why not share it with the world? Let more people discover this piece by sharing it on social media and by word-of-mouth.

Connect with me
Want more? Get in touch with me and let's interact. send me an email via
author.isaacessilfie@gmail.com

BOOKS BY ISAAC ESSILFIE

Incorruptible Series:

➤ Incorruptible Book #1: The realm of the mind

➤ Incorruptible Book #2: Steadfast & immovable amidst the darkness of this present world

Daily Glory Series:

➤ How to Pray: The dimensions of operation in prayer

➤ How to walk in grace and favour daily

➤ Manifesting your heavenly inheritance

➤ Loving by loving yourself

➤ The Spirit of Christ

➤ The New Creature: Life from Death

➤ Immune to Disease: Enjoying divine health and healing

ABOUT THE AUTHOR

Isaac Essilfie is a Christian Nonfiction author.

Writing is one of his hobbies. He is passionate about helping people create a beautiful living atmosphere. This is what has inspired him to write many books to engage more people.

He also writes to reach out to people with the saving knowledge of Christ.

When he is not writing, he is catching up on the latest animation, action and horror movies.

Printed in Great Britain
by Amazon